Community

LIVING AS THE PEOPLE OF GOD

Scott Nelson

Foreword by Alan Hirsch

FORGE GUIDES FOR MISSIONAL CONVERSATION

IVP Connect

An imprint of InterVarsity Press
Downers Grove, Illinois

InterVarsity Press
P.O. Box 1400, Downers Grove, IL 60515-1426
World Wide Web: www.ivpress.com
E-mail: email@ivpress.com

InterVarsity Press® is the book-publishing division of InterVarsity Christian Fellowship/USA®, a movement of students and faculty active on campus at hundreds of universities, colleges and schools of nursing in the United States of America, and a member movement of the International Fellowship of Evangelical Students. For information about local and regional activities, write Public Relations Dept., InterVarsity Christian Fellowship/USA, 6400 Schroeder Rd., P.O. Box 7895, Madison, WI 53707-7895, or visit the IVCF website at <www.intervarsity.org>.

All Scripture quotations, unless otherwise indicated, are taken from the Holy Bible, New International Version®, NIV® *Copyright © 1973, 1978, 1984, 2011 by Biblica, Inc.™ Used by permission. All rights reserved worldwide.*

While all stories in this book are true, some names and identifying information in this book have been changed to protect the privacy of the individuals involved.

Cover design: Cindy Kiple
Interior design: Beth Hagenberg

ISBN 978-0-8308-1048-2 (print)
ISBN 978-0-8308-9570-0 (digital)

Printed in the United States of America ∞

Library of Congress Cataloging-in Publication Data
A catalog record for this book is available from the Library of Congress.

| P | 20 | 19 | 18 | 17 | 16 | 15 | 14 | 13 | 12 | 11 | 10 | 9 | 8 | 7 | 6 | 5 | 4 | 3 | 2 | 1 |
| Y | 30 | 29 | 28 | 27 | 26 | 25 | 24 | 23 | 22 | 21 | 20 | 19 | 18 | 17 | 16 | 15 | 14 | 13 |

CONTENTS

FOREWORD

For the better part of two decades now, *missional* has been equal parts buzzword and byword in the contemporary church.

Many church leaders have decried the trendiness of the term, predicting that it will eventually go the way of all fads, and that responsible church leadership involves simply waiting it out, keeping the faith. And it's hard to deny the trendiness of the term: as the editors of *Leadership Journal* noted in their preface to an article of mine five years ago, "A quick search on Google uncovers the presence of 'missional communities,' 'missional leaders,' 'missional worship,' even 'missional seating,' and 'missional coffee.'"[1] The closer the application of the term approaches absurdity, the less seriously we are inclined to take it.

And yet over the same period the concept of a missional church has proved its durability. Conference after conference has organized itself around the concept that God is on mission in the world, and that as means to the end of achieving his mission God has created a church. Seminary after seminary has reconfigured its core curricula to take the model of a church on mission seriously, and to train pastors and other leaders to understand themselves as missionaries first, "keepers" of the faith a distant second. What so many have dismissed as a fad or a trend, substantial and growing numbers of people are recognizing as a paradigm shift.

Of course, any number of paradigm-shifting conversations are taking place at the conceptual level among the leadership of the global church at any given moment. Many such conversations bubble up only to dissipate; such in-house deliberation is part of the long history of the faith. It is in this historical reality that the durability and trajectory of the missional church conversation reveals its significance. More than a mere theoretical conversation, the missional church bears the marks of a true movement—broad-based, but with a cohesive sense of self-understanding; goal-driven, but deeply rooted in principles and conviction; critical of the status quo, yet always motivated by the greater good. Christianity itself has always been a movement, inspired by the God who created the world and called it good, who so loved the world that he gave his only Son for it.

Any movement over time has the capacity to atrophy, to be distracted by its own sense of self-preservation, to be enthralled by the beauty of its past accomplishments and the currency of its cultural power. But the original vision of the movement relentlessly beckons, confronting our self-congratulation and propelling us toward the greater good of our original calling.

At Forge we have always said that the best critique of the bad is the practice of the better. With this series of guides on missional practices we are trying to help create a more productive and better future for a church now in systemic decline. We believe the church was made for far more than mere self-preservation, and certainly not for retreat. We were made to be a highly transformative Jesus movement; we had best get on with being that. To do this we need to redisciple the church into its calling and mission. Discipleship is a huge key, and for this we need tools.

Every movement requires the education—the *formation*—of its people. I believe the next phase of the movement that is the missional church resides not so much in seminaries or elder meetings as around the tables of people of faith wherever they find themselves. These Forge Guides for Missional Conversation are intended to facilitate those conversations—to help you, wherever you are, to step together into the flow of God's mission in the world.

Scott Nelson is particularly equipped to facilitate such conversations. He has held leadership positions in traditional churches and studied the church's mission while pursuing his doctorate. He has taken on the responsibility of the theological direction of Forge Mission Training Network in America even as he has developed a missional community in the neighborhood where he lives. The mission of God is thoroughly integrated into Scott's life—heart and soul, mind and strength—which is as it is intended to be.

Each of the five guides that make up this series will be valuable on its own; thoroughly scriptural, accessibly theological, highly practical and fundamentally spiritual, each will give you a fuller appreciation of what it means to be a follower of Jesus on God's mission. Taken together, however, they are a sort of curriculum for a movement: you and your friends will be fully equipped for every good work that God has in mind for you in the place where you find yourself.

Our missionary God created a church in service to his mission. We were made for a movement. Read on if you're ready to move!

Alan Hirsch

INTRODUCTION
TO THE FORGE GUIDES

I've been obsessed with the idea of helping Christians develop a missionary imagination for their daily lives ever since I began to develop such an imagination back in 2007. My missionary imagination began at a church staff retreat. I was asked what I thought our church staff should do if God dropped us all from a helicopter into our city with absolutely no resources and asked us to start a church. While thinking of my answer to this question, I realized I would have to take on the mindset of a missionary—go out to the people, learn who they are, get involved in their lives, care about what they care about. The years that have passed since that fateful question have been an amazing journey for me. I quit my job, dove into full-time study of the missionary mindset in Christian congregations, began exploring ways to live like a missionary in the condominium complex where my wife and I currently live, and teamed up with the Forge America Mission Training Network to be a part of an organization that actively seeks to implant a missionary mindset in Christians and their faith communities.

I've written these guides to help you ask some of the same questions that I asked, and to help you think about what it might look like if you, your group or your church were to develop a missionary imagination for everyday living. There are at least three reasons why it is crucially important that you ask these questions and develop a missionary imagination.

The first reason is the cultural changes that are taking place in Western contexts. Changes such as increasing globalization, religious and cultural pluralism, huge advances in science and technology, the collapse of many modern principles and the growth of postmodernism, and the secularization of the West have drastically altered many cultural landscapes. If the gospel is to be proclaimed faithfully and effectively in these changing contexts, Christians must be missionaries who study cultures in order to translate the gospel so that all can clearly hear it. Simply saying and doing the same things in the same ways as generations past is no longer effective.

A second reason it is vitally important for Christians to develop a missionary mindset is the crisis facing the institutional church. The many different statistical studies that measure the size and influence of the church in the United States are sobering. Despite the explosion of megachurches, congregations in the United States as a whole consist of older people and fewer participants, and experience decreased influence in local contexts. The institutional, established church is experiencing a serious internal crisis as contexts change and congregations fail to adapt. Christians must regain a sense of their missionary calling if the trend of a diminishing role for the Christian faith is to be reversed in the West.

Third, I see evidence of a common longing for a deeper, lived-out faith among many Christians, especially among emerging generations. I've felt it and so have many others who I have read and talked with. It is the feeling that something about the way I am participating in church and faith seems to be missing; it seems to be too easy or too shallow. Conversations with Christians across the country reveal a longing to be challenged, to do something significant with their faith, to make a difference in the lives of people both globally and locally. By developing a missionary imagination for everyday living, these Christians develop a mindset that can lead to deeper expressions of faith, which ultimately reorient a person's whole life around what God is doing and wants to do in this world.

My life story and the three reasons I just listed compelled me to write and use these conversation guides for my own small group. Perhaps you have had a similar experience, or maybe one of the three reasons prompted you to pick up the guides. Even if not, I sincerely hope the questions contained in these guides will infect your minds, as they did mine. And I sincerely hope the mission of God will infect your lives, as I pray every day for it to infect mine.

USING THE FORGE GUIDES

My focus in creating these guides has not been to give you all the answers. I firmly believe you and the members of your group need to discern the answers for yourselves, and further, to generate the creativity that will shape your imagination for what a missionary lifestyle might look like in your life and community. My task in creating these guides is to help you ask good questions.

While creating these guides, I kept coming back to the idea of minimalist running shoes. The science behind these increasingly popular shoes claims that the human body is naturally equipped to run. Big, cushiony, fancy running shoes are not only unnecessary but counterproductive. What runners really need is a simple shoe that accentuates their natural abilities, encourages proper running form and protects their feet from environmental hazards.

These guides are designed to be a lot like minimalist running shoes. They offer the bare minimum you will need to ask good questions, seek innovative answers and develop a new imagination. The guides do not do the work for you. Rather, let them draw out your natural ability to hear from Scripture, to think about the world around you, to wonder about who God is and to imagine ways you can live as a missionary.

These four practices appear in each lesson under the headings

"Dwelling in the Word," "Contextual Analysis," "Theological Reflection" and "Missionary Imagination." I have identified relevant biblical texts, but it is your job to listen for how God is speaking to you and your group. The guides also provide probing questions about your local context, but it is your job to do the analysis required to provide the answers. Similarly, the guides will provide theological content and point to basic principles of missional living, but it is your job to reflect on the nature of God and how he is asking you to live out his mission in your context.

To help you understand what you will be doing as you work through the conversation guides, a brief description of each basic practice follows. Please note that some groups will naturally gravitate to some of the practices more than to others. Don't feel the need to go through each section with a fine-toothed comb. There is more material than will likely be needed for most group gatherings, so be flexible with the practices and allow the group to choose how much time to allocate to each section.

Practice 1: Dwelling in the Word

Each group gathering begins with a time to hear from Scripture through communal reading and listening.[2] Dwelling in the same text over a period of six weeks (or more!) will allow your group to begin developing a shared imagination and a shared openness to the many things God may want to say and do through the text.

The group listens to the passage, reflects in silence for a few moments and then breaks into pairs to discuss two questions about the text. After sufficient time has passed (while allowing adequate time for the remainder of the session), the group gathers together. Individuals share what their partners heard in the text while answers are recorded. This section concludes with the group asking, What might God be up to in this passage for us today?

Sometimes people will doubt the value of returning to the same text time after time, but trust the process and believe that the Bible is the living Word of God. The more you continue to return to the same text, the more you will find blessing at the insight you gain, the habits you learn, the imagination you develop and the community you form.

One final point can help you get started on the right foot: dwelling in the Word is about hearing from God's Word and hearing from each other. Each person is responsible for helping one other person give voice to what she or he heard from the text and to then be an advocate for that person's thoughts in the larger group. These practices are intended to help the group create an environment where thoughts are safely shared and members listen deeply to one another. Over time, dwelling in the Word is a powerful tool that can form a community of the Spirit where the presence and power of the Spirit is both welcome and expected.

Practice 2: Contextual Analysis

Missionaries know that the gospel must be translated—literally and figuratively—into local contexts. Every local culture is unique and will hear and receive the gospel in different ways. A good missionary learns to understand local cultures so that he or she can inculturate the gospel in a way specifically tailored to a specific people group. At times of inculturation into new contexts, the gospel has proven to be the most effective at bringing about radical transformation in individuals, communities and whole societies. The Forge Guides for Missional Conversation are designed to help Christian communities inculturate and translate the gospel into their local contexts by facilitating shared practices of contextual analysis during group gatherings.

Practices of contextual analysis will focus on three main areas: describing the local context, discerning what God is already doing in the local context and wondering together what God might want to do in the local context. A variety of ways to practice contextual analysis are provided in each session. Sometimes the group will simply have questions to answer. At other times they will be asked to complete an activity or reflect personally. It is hoped that the variety of practices provided will lead the group to a new understanding of their context and will help the group faithfully proclaim and live out the gospel in new and exciting ways that transform the members of the group and the world around them.

Practice 3: Theological Reflection

David Kelsey defines theology as the search to understand and know God truly.[3] Theology in this sense becomes wisdom in relationship to God. Much like understanding an instruction manual about building a bike leads to the ability to build that bike, searching to understand God brings about some ability to relate with God through spiritual practices, worship and faith. Those who know God can sense and participate in what God is doing in the world around them.

The section on theological reflection is designed to help your group seek to know God truly so that the group might become wise in relationship to God. It will encourage you to actively wonder about who God is and what he is up to in the world. Scripture passages and a few reflection questions will be provided for the group to study. Sometimes other sources of theological reflection—such as distinct church traditions, church history or other texts—will be provided. No matter what specific content is provided for you to reflect on, the goal will always be the same and that is for your group to ask, What can we know about who God is and what God does? How does this influence the way we relate to God and join with him in what he is doing?

Practice 4: Missionary Imagination

Each session will conclude with a time for developing a missionary imagination through conversation, personal reflection, group affirmation, prayer or a variety of other activities. The time set aside for missionary imagination is intended to help each individual in the group gain a better sense of his or her own missionary calling, and also to help the group as a whole develop a missionary imagination for its existence. I've tried particularly hard to provide a wide variety of activities in this section. The goal of these activities as well as their very nature is meant to help you and your group break the mold when it comes to calling, vision and imagination. When my own small group went through this material, we had a blast doing things like drawing pictures, sharing stories, writing limericks and making collages, as well as answering the more conventional discussion questions. Have fun with this section and do your best to encourage one another to be imaginative, innovative and experimental in missionary living.

Before We Meet Again

Midweek assignments are given at the end of each week's session. These assignments are fun little projects designed to help group members continue to think about the session throughout the week. For instance, one assignment might ask members to take pictures of three things during the week that they think represent the work of God in the world. Time for the group to review the midweek assignment is often built into the next week's session. I strongly encourage your group to complete these assignments whenever possible. My own group really enjoyed them!

Recording and Reflecting

As your group talks through these guides, my final recommendation is to take notes during the discussions, whether individually or through a general secretary. These records will help you discern patterns and commonalities that may help you see what God is doing in your lives.

INTRODUCTION

The Missionary Nature of the Church

I have the distinct privilege of working for Forge America, a mission training network that helps Christians develop a missionary imagination for their lives and their churches. Part of my role with Forge includes traveling to our various residency programs in cities across the United States to teach residents about the missional church movement. One of the first things I teach is my belief that the church needs to shift from being an event-driven place to being a mission-driven community. This guide is the outworking of that belief.

In most of my experiences, the way Christians talk about and act as the church reflects a deep internal understanding of the church as a place that houses a very significant event. Think about it. People say they are "going to church," which means they are headed to a building or gathering place or, more specifically, that they are headed to a worship service at that building or gathering place. I'd be willing to bet that you have heard someone ask, "How was church?"—by which they mean, "How was the worship gathering you attended?" This language reveals a fundamental understanding of the church as a certain event that happens at a particular place.

Much of the Christian behavior that I have witnessed also belies an image of the church as an event-driven place. For most of my Christian life the defining action of many Christians, including myself, has been gathering on Sundays for worship. Christian faithfulness throughout the week is, of course, also encouraged, but most energy is spent maintaining a quality worship experience on Sunday mornings and getting as many people as possible to come and participate. This approach to being the church dominated my own imagination through my high school and college years and carried through into my first years of ministry in a local church. As a staff, our time, energy and resources went toward gathering people in our building, mostly for worship on Sunday mornings, but occasionally for various events throughout the week as well. Unconsciously, we operated almost entirely as an event-driven place.

I greatly appreciate my Christian upbringing and remember fondly the many brothers and sisters in Christ who have surrounded me throughout my life. I cannot help but look back, though, and see how our imagination for what God might have wanted to do with us was limited by our understanding of what it meant to be church. I cannot help but wonder what me missed because we were working so hard to establish our places and run our events. Part of what we missed out on is the missionary nature of the church; we missed out on living as a mission-driven community because we were too focused on being an event-driven place.

Much has been written in the last half century about the missionary nature of the church. Consider the following statements:

- "The pilgrim Church is missionary by her very nature, since it is from the mission of the Son and the mission of the Holy Spirit that she draws her origin, in accordance with the decree of God the Father." (Vatican II, *Ad Gentes* 2)

- "The church exists by mission as fire exists by burning." (H. Emil Brunner, *The Word in the World*)

These are just two thoughts among many that are helping to ignite a movement to develop a new image of the church, one that breaks out of the mold of the church as building, place or event. The new image is more dynamic, picturing not a building but a people, not a place but a movement, not an event but a community and lifestyle. The new image sees the church as created by the mission of God to live for the mission of God as the people of God in every place where God sends them to live.

A friend told me about a time when he was the pastor of a church plant that had grown to over twelve hundred members. The church was very much aligned to the event-driven model, so much so that he said that if he were to meet an actor, his first thought would be, *How can I get her to join the church's drama team?* My friend eventually had a "missional conversion" and began to change the way he thought about the church. He eventually planted another church in Hollywood, where he was constantly meeting actors. Then, instead of wondering how he could get the actors to join his drama teams, he wondered how he could get his church to join those actors in mission to their friends, family and colleagues. How could his church help these actors live on mission in the acting community where they lived their lives? These are incredibly different approaches to being the church together!

I've had a "missional conversion" of my own and am now exploring ways to live out a new imagination, both personally and with my brothers and sisters in Christ. The six sessions in this conversation guide represent the images of the church that are helping me rework my imagination. Each session pairs a different image of the church with a different practice found in missional churches. I hope this coupling will prove fruitful to you as you explore the missionary nature of the church and seek to understand how you might participate in or help to form a missional community.

_____

LIVING AS GOD'S ELECT

*You yourselves have seen what
I did to Egypt, and how I carried you
on eagles' wings and brought you to myself. Now if
you obey me fully and keep my covenant, then out of all
nations you will be my treasured possession. Although
the whole earth is mine, you will be for me a
kingdom of priests and a holy nation.*

Exodus 19:4-6, emphasis added

*The "people of God" in all ages have been one.
Together they have been called to the same privilege of
service and ministry on behalf of the coming Man of Promise.
All were to be agents of God's blessing to all on earth.
Nothing could be clearer from the missionary and
ministry call issued in Exodus 19:4-6.*

Walter Kaiser, *Mission in the Old Testament*

Election and mission go together. If the church is God's elect people, then the church is elected to mission. To be the church is to be the people of God, to be the people of God is to be God's elect, and to be God's elect is to be God's chosen instrument for his mission. The church is missionary by nature, a missionary community, a missional people. This has been the case from the very beginning of God's history with his people.

Dwelling in the Word

- Begin in prayer, inviting the Spirit to guide your group as you dwell in the text.
- Read aloud 1 Peter 2:4-12.
- After the reading has been completed, allow a few moments of silence to reflect on the passage and what stands out to you.
- Break into pairs (preferably with someone you don't know well) and discuss the following questions. Use this time to practice listening to each other as well as to the text.
  - What in the text captured your imagination?
  - What question would you most like to ask a biblical scholar?
- Gather once again as a large group and share your partners' responses.
- Review these responses and discuss: What might God be up to in the passage for us today?

Contextual Analysis

In Exodus 19:4-6 God reminds his people that he acted in mighty ways to bring them out of Egypt in order that they might be his special people, appointed to be a kingdom of priests and a holy nation, a people set apart to live for God's purposes. His people were freed so that they might reveal God to the nations around them.

Assume that God acted in mighty ways to form your group. Why did God form you?

1. To what context does God want to reveal himself through you? To whom has God sent you or your group?

2. Within your context, what are the prevailing thoughts about the following:

   • God

   • Church

   • God's involvement with the world (past, present, future)

   • If you could change how your context views any of these things, what changes would you make?

Theological Reflection: *The God Who Calls, Gathers and Sends His People*

To be the people of God means that the church is "that historic community whose origin stemmed from God's covenant promises and whose pilgrimage had been sustained by God's call."[4] When the Bible refers to the nation of Israel or the church as the people of God, it is noting that the very existence of God's people is based on God's purpose, promise and calling. To be the people of God is to be called, gathered together and sent on mission by God—the One who calls, gathers and sends his people to accomplish his redemptive purposes.

3. Read 1 Peter 2:4-12. List all the ways the author describes the church. Next to each description, write what you think the description signifies or means.

4. Look particularly at 1 Peter 2:9-10. Compare it to Exodus 19:4-6 (and what you know about the story of the exodus). How is the church in the New Testament like the Hebrew people who were freed from slavery in Egypt?

5. What does 1 Peter 2:4-12 (and its comparison to Exodus 19) teach you about God: Who he is, how he works, what he is up to in the world?

6. The phrase "I will be your God and you will be my people" (or something similar) occurs multiple times throughout the Bible. Break into pairs and read a few examples, scanning the surrounding verses for context: Exodus 6:7; Leviticus 26:12; Deuteronomy 26:16-19; 29:9-14; Jeremiah 24:7. What is the significance of this relationship between God and his people? What does it mean to God and require of him? What does it mean to the people and require of them?

Missionary Imagination: *Discerning Missional Vocation*

Vocation (from the Latin *vocatio*, "to call") is experiencing and living by a calling. The vocation of the church is, therefore, related to its calling. "For the church to understand itself to be missional ("sent") is to discern its vocation ("calling"). To be called by God is to be taken into a way of life and mission."[5] The way of life that defines the church constantly discerns the missional calling God has issued to the church both universally and locally. The church embodies the universal mission of God in a local way as a witness to the surrounding context that it belongs to God and no other.

7. What would it mean for your group to understand itself as the people of God elected for mission? What sense of vocation might this give you?

8. "The Church is the community of people called by God who, through the Holy Spirit, are united with Jesus Christ and sent as disciples to bear witness to God's reconciliation, healing and transformation of creation."[6] Discuss how well this definition of the church defines your group. Does the description of the church's vocation match your own sense of vocation?

9. Missional communities develop practices that allow the community to actively discern the specific missional vocation God has given to the community.[7] How well does your group do this? How might you improve in your communal discernment of God's missional call for your group?

10. The following covenant/confession is offered by Darrell Guder as an example of the common understanding and sense of vocation to which the members of a missional community might commit:

> We believe that we are the church, that is, we are a community of God's people called and set apart for witness to the good news of Jesus Christ. We are blessed to be a blessing. As the Father has sent Christ, so Christ sends us. Jesus Christ has defined us as his witnesses where we are. We believe therefore that the Holy Spirit not only calls us but also enables and gifts us for that mission. Our task is to determine

the particular focus and direction of our mission. We are to identify the charisms given us by the Spirit for mission. We have the responsibility and the capacity, through the Holy Spirit, to shape ourselves for faithful witness. Our purpose defines our organizational structures—which means that our mission challenges us to re-form our structures so that we can be faithful in our witness.[8]

As a group, draft your own covenant/confession that highlights your current sense of missional vocation. You will update this covenant throughout your conversations in this guide.

11. Using Legos, Kinnex, blocks or any other type of toy that allows you to build structures, together construct a model of the church as a missional community that discerns its missional vocation. You will update this structure each session, so keep it in a safe place if possible.

Before We Meet Again

- Continue to read and reflect on 1 Peter 2:4-12 or any other passage from this week's conversation. Record your thoughts here:

- Continue to study the image of the church as the elect people of God by reading paragraphs 9-18 of "The Nature and Mission of the

Church" by the World Council of Churches (available online; search Nature+Mission+Church). You will find recommendations for additional resources at the end of this guide.

- Write, draw or build something that represents your current understanding of the missional vocation of your church or group. Be prepared to share this at your group's next meeting.

LIVING AS FOREIGNERS
AND PILGRIMS

For here we do not have an enduring city,
but we are looking for the city that is to come.

Hebrews 13:14

Our citizenship is in heaven. And we eagerly await a
Savior from there, the Lord Jesus Christ, who, by the power that
enables him to bring everything under his control, will transform
our lowly bodies so that they will be like his glorious body.

Philippians 3:20-21

The people of God are pilgrims on a journey toward the Promised Land of God: "The nature of the Church is never to be fully defined in static terms, but only in terms of that to which it is going. It cannot be understood rightly except in a perspective which is at once missionary and eschatological."[9]

Living as foreigners and pilgrims in the present world drives the church to always have an eager expectation of the world that is to come. The life of the church is defined by a sojourn through this world toward the promised future of God, living in the world but never making the world its home.

Share any thoughts or reflections from the assignments at the end of session 1.

Dwelling in the Word

- Begin in prayer, inviting the Spirit to guide your group as you dwell in the text.

- Read aloud 1 Peter 2:4-12.

- After the reading has been completed, allow a few moments of silence to reflect on the passage and what stands out to you.

- Break into pairs (preferably with someone you don't know well) and discuss the following questions. Use this time to practice listening to each other as well as to the text.

  - What in the text captured your imagination?

  - What question would you most like to ask a biblical scholar?

- Gather once again as a large group and share your partners' responses.

- Review these responses and discuss: What might God be up to in the passage for us today?

Contextual Analysis

1. Look at your previous identification of the context God has sent you to (see session 1, question 1). Try to make your answer more specific or narrow if possible. Name specific people and places.

2. What about your local context do you think reflects the world as God desires it to be? What goes against God's desires for the world?

3. What do people in your context believe about the future? What do they think the world will be like in five, ten and fifty years?

4. What changes do you think would take place if the people in your context put their hope fully in the reign of God?

Theological Reflection: *The God Who Guides His People Toward the Future*

The World Council of Churches asked some scholars to study the nature and mission of the church. They came to understand the church as unsettled, saying, "Throughout the ages, the Church of God continues the way of pilgrimage to the eternal rest prepared for it (cf. Heb 4:9-11). It is a prophetic sign of the fulfillment God will bring about through Christ by the power of the Spirit."[10]

5. Where in the Bible or the history of the church do you see the people of God functioning as foreigners? As pilgrims?

6. How has God guided his people throughout history?

7. Break into pairs and read 2 Corinthians 4:13–5:10, Philippians 3:12–4:1 and Hebrews 11:1–12:3. How do these texts define a pilgrim mindset? What do they teach about God?

8. In *Community in Mission*, Phil Needham calls the church "a band of pilgrims who are called to separate themselves from the oppressive patterns of the present world order and to keep moving toward the possibilities which the new Kingdom in Christ offers."[11] How do you think a church of foreigners and pilgrims should relate to God? How should that church understand its mission?

Missionary Imagination: *Pointing Toward the Reign of God*

A defining characteristic of missional congregations is that they have a sense of something bigger than themselves. Their very life as a local congregation is bound up in the bigger sense of God's reign. A community centered on mission seeks first God's kingdom (Mt 6) and in so doing lives in such a way that the rest of the world sees what the coming kingdom will look like. The missional church

> lives within God's redemptive reign, the church lives between the times of the introduction of the blessing of the Spirit and the final judgment of sin. In this position, the church is a clear demonstration to the world that heaven has already begun. From this position, God uses the church as a sign, foretaste, and instrument to invite all humanity and creation to come to know fully the living and true God.[12]

9. How might your group take up the foreigner-pilgrim identity of the people of God?

10. The *Treasure in Clay Jars* report indicated that one of the "hallmarks of missional congregations" is the "recognition that the church itself is an incomplete expression of the reign of God."[13] How can your group be a pointer toward God's reign for your local context?

11. Update the model you built during session 1 of the church as a missional community. What needs to be added to the model? Taken away? Modified?

12. Rewrite, add to or change the covenant you wrote in session 1 as you see fit, based on the conversation you had during this session.

Before We Meet Again

- Continue to read and reflect on 1 Peter 2:4-12 or any other passage from this week's conversation. Record your thoughts here:

- Write a short story about a pilgrim journey toward God. The journey can be your own, that of your group, somebody you know or a fictional character. Use your short story to depict how a foreigner/pilgrim lifestyle can help the church live as a missional community. Record your story here or on a separate piece of paper.

- Continue to study the image of the church as the pilgrim people of God by reading paragraphs 19, 43-47 of "The Nature and Mission of the Church" by the World Council of Churches (available online) and *Ad Gentes*, a document from Vatican II (available online; search Ad+Gentes). You can find recommendations for additional resources at the end of this guide.

- Read (or begin to read) Exodus through Joshua in the Old Testament at a pace that is comfortable yet challenging for you. As you read, ask yourself, What does it look like to be a foreign, exodus people on pilgrimage toward God's promise?

LIVING AS THE
BODY OF CHRIST

One of the most powerful images related to the church in the New Testament is that of the body of Christ. The image is powerful because it makes the gospel of Christ a reality. Much as Christ was God-made-flesh, the church is the gospel-made-flesh, a physical reality where the kingdom of God rules on earth and can be seen, felt and experienced. Essentially, the church is where heaven meets earth.

For this reason some have called the church the "tangible kingdom," "the hermeneutic of the gospel" or the "gospel materialized." Paul Minear sees the body of Christ—with Christ as the head and the church as the interdependent parts—as "a way of describing a social revolution. A new society had appeared that transformed the criteria of social judgment, the bases of social cohesion, and the structures of social institutions."[14] Craig Van Gelder says that the "very existence" of the body of Christ "demonstrates that [God's] redemptive reign has already begun."[15]

Demonstration plots are used in farming to introduce new developments to the farmers who will have to use them in the future. New innovations are applied to a small parcel of land. If farmers like what the plot of land demonstrates, they will take up the innovation. In a similar way, Van Gelder suggests, the church is God's demonstration plot. "Its very presence invites the world to watch, listen, examine, and consider accepting God's reign as a superior way of living."[16]

Share your thoughts and reflections from session 2.

Dwelling in the Word

- Begin in prayer, inviting the Spirit to guide your group as you dwell in the text.

- Read aloud 1 Peter 2:4-12.

- After the reading has been completed, allow a few moments of silence to reflect on the passage and what stands out to you.

- Break into pairs (preferably with someone you don't know well) and discuss the following questions. Use this time to practice listening to each other as well as to the text.

  - What in the text captured your imagination?

  - What question would you most like to ask a biblical scholar?

- Gather once again as a large group and share your partners' responses.

- Review these responses and discuss: What might God be up to in the passage for us today?

Contextual Analysis

1. Begin by naming, defining and describing your local mission context as you did in the previous two sessions. Be as specific as

possible and list as many details and descriptors of your context as you can.

2. If the church is the body of Christ, what body would your local context be? What or who is the head of your local context? What is required to be a member or part of the body?

3. When the people in your local context look at the church, what do you think they see? Do they see a demonstration plot of God's intent for the world? A social revolution? Or something different? Why?

Theological Reflection: *The God Who Unites His People Under His Reign*

4. Break into pairs and read Ephesians 1:22–2:22; 4:1-16; 5:1-5, 22-33; and Colossians 1:15-23; 2:6-23. What do you learn about Christ as the head of the church? What do you learn about the church as united under Christ?

5. Read 1 Corinthians 12 and Romans 12. What do you learn about the church as one body united under Christ?

Missionary Imagination: *Practices That Demonstrate God's Intent for the World*

Missional communities understand that one of the important parts of living for God's mission is the way members act toward one another under the lordship of Christ. These communities understand that they are where the "gospel proclamation materializes, that is, where it can be seen, felt, heard, and tasted."[17] Missional communities demonstrate the intent God has for the world through a new way of living toward God and one another.

6. What communal practices do you think most demonstrate God's intent for the world?

7. Bonhoeffer wrote the following in *Life Together:*

> When God was merciful, when He revealed Jesus Christ to us as our Brother, when He won our hearts by His love, this was the beginning of our instruction in divine love. When God was merciful to us, we learned to be merciful with [one another]. When we received forgiveness instead of judgment, we, too, were made ready to forgive [each other]. *What God did to us, we then owed to others. . . . Thus God Himself taught us to meet one another as God has met us in Christ.*[18]

Through Christ, God revealed to the church his intent for how humans were to relate to him and to one another. Based on what God did for you, what do you owe others? Based on how God has met you in Christ, how ought you meet one another?

8. Based on what you know about your group, your context and the instructions for Christian community found in the Bible, how do you think your group can best demonstrate God's intent for the world to your context?

9. Use the concepts and ideas you just discussed to update your model of the church as a missional community. What needs to be added to the model? Taken away? Modified?

10. Rewrite, add to or change your covenant as you see fit based on the conversation you had during this session.

Before We Meet Again

- Continue to read and reflect on 1 Peter 2:4-12 or any other passage from this week's conversation. Record your thoughts here:

- Do something to bless two or three people in your group this week. Be intentional about showing love to them as a way of developing a pattern of life that demonstrates God's intent for the world.

- Continue to study the image of the church as the body of Christ by reading paragraphs 20-21 of "The Nature and Mission of the Church" by the World Council of Churches (available online). You will find recommendations for additional resources at the end of this guide.

LIVING AS THE TEMPLE OF THE HOLY SPIRIT

Mission is first and foremost an affair not of words and activities but of presence—the presence of God in the midst of God's people and the presence of God's people in the midst of humanity.

James Chukwuma Okoye,
Israel and the Nations

When we encounter the church, we move into spiritual territory that occupies earthly terrain. We encounter the living God in the midst of our humanity. We encounter the Spirit of God dwelling in the midst of a people who are created and formed into a unique community.

Craig Van Gelder,
The Essence of the Church

God has always given his presence to his people. In fact, the story of Scripture can be told based on where God's people are in relation to his presence. God's presence came in a dramatic new way through Jesus Christ, who—through his merging of heaven and earth—made it possible for the Spirit of God to live in his followers. The Spirit of God is the presence of God that powers the church to live as a community on mission with and for God. Missional communities depend on the Holy Spirit to empower them, and they recognize that God's presence is often revealed to their contexts through them.

Share how you blessed others or were blessed by others since session 3.

Dwelling in the Word

- Begin in prayer, inviting the Spirit to guide your group as you dwell in the text.

- Read aloud 1 Peter 2:4-12.

- After the reading has been completed, allow a few moments of silence to reflect on the passage and what stands out to you.

- Break into pairs (preferably with someone you don't know well) and discuss the following questions. Use this time to practice listening to each other as well as to the text.

  - What in the text captured your imagination?

  - What question would you most like to ask a biblical scholar?

- Gather once again as a large group and share your partners' responses.

- Review these responses and discuss: What might God be up to in the passage for us today?

Contextual Analysis

1. If a person from another country moved into your local context

with the desire to live like a missionary, what is the single most valuable piece of information you would tell him or her?

Theological Reflection: *The God Who Indwells His People*

2. Read Romans 8:1-17. What is the outcome when the Spirit lives in the believer(s)?

3. Break into pairs and read 1 Corinthians 3:16-17; 6:15-19; Ephesians 2:17-22; or 1 Peter 2:5. What is significant about the church as a temple of the Holy Spirit? What does this teach about God? About the church? About mission?

4. Come back together as a group and read Paul's sermon in Acts 17:22-31. How does Paul's sermon describe God in relation to the temple and the church? How does Paul depict the church as the temple of the Holy Spirit?

Missionary Imagination: *Dependence on the Holy Spirit*

The researchers who compiled the report on missional congregations for *Treasure in Clay Jars* discovered that the missional congregations they studied all displayed a deep dependence on the Holy Spirit. This dependence on the Holy Spirit was displayed most prominently through their times of corporate prayer, but was also seen in the language used on a regular basis throughout the various congregations. The mindset these congregations had in common held that "The missional church is incapable of fulfilling its call, save for guidance from the Spirit of God and for the Spirit's empowerment of the church's witness."[19]

5. To what extent does your group depend on the Holy Spirit? What would your lives look like if you lived as a group dependent on the Spirit? What practices ought to be regular patterns in your group?

6. Spend a significant amount of time praying with one another for the presence of the Spirit to sustain and empower your group, and for God to increase your dependence on the Spirit.

7. Encourage each other by telling one another ways you see the Spirit at work in each other and in the group as a whole.

8. Use the concepts you just discussed to update your model of the church as a missional community. What needs to be added to the model? Taken away? Modified?

9. Rewrite, add to or change the covenant of your group as you see fit based on the conversation you had during this session.

Before We Meet Again

- Continue to read and reflect on 1 Peter 2:4-12 or any other passage from this week's conversation. Record your thoughts here:

- Spend a significant amount of time in prayer every day for the power of the Spirit to be present in your life and for your ability to depend on the Spirit on a daily basis.

- Continue to study the image of the church as the temple of the Holy Spirit by reading paragraphs 22-23 of "The Nature and Mission of the Church" by the World Council of Churches (available online). You will find recommendations for additional resources at the end of this guide.

LIVING AS
THE NEW CREATION

It is rare to find stories that are new in a completely unexpected way. On the rare occasion that a truly new story does pop up, I find myself completely engrossed. Movies like *The Matrix* or books like *Ender's Game* by Orson Scott Card create worlds beyond our imagination, inviting us to let loose for a brief moment and envision a new way of being.

The church of God offers the world exactly that type of brand new story. A new way has been opened to God through Jesus Christ, and a new kind of living toward God and one another is now possible. That new life is defined by the power and presence of the Holy Spirit within each follower of Christ and within every community of followers. Those indwelled by the Spirit no longer live by the patterns of the world. They love as Jesus loved and live as Jesus lived. They are a new kind of people living a new kind of story.

Missional congregations share this identity as the new creation of the Holy Spirit. They understand that their identity, motivation, vocation and character are wrapped up in the mission of God. They rely on the Spirit to empower them to participate in God's mission and know that their very existence will be a light in the darkness, a contrast community, a new creation in a world where very little is ever truly new. As a new creation missional congregations show the world who God is, what his love looks like and where his plans are leading.

Share your thoughts and reflections since session 4.

Dwelling in the Word

- Begin in prayer, inviting the Spirit to guide your group as you dwell in the text.
- Read aloud 1 Peter 2:4-12.
- After the reading has been completed, allow a few moments of silence to reflect on the passage and what stands out to you.
- Break into pairs (preferably with someone you don't know well) and discuss the following questions. Use this time to practice listening to each other as well as to the text.
  - What in the text captured your imagination?
  - What question would you most like to ask a biblical scholar?
- Gather once again as a large group and share your partners' responses.
- Review these responses and discuss: What might God be up to in the passage for us today?

Contextual Analysis

1. What is the greatest single threat your context poses to the person or group desiring to live on mission within it?

2. What is the greatest single opportunity your context offers to the person or group desiring to live on mission within it?

3. Can you think of examples of people or groups who have been derailed by or have succumbed to the threats within your context? Who have seized the opportunities with great success?

Theological Reflection: *The God Who Creates a New Kind of People*

The church is the new creation of God, a community designed to be a new kind of people, formed by a new command, dead and raised to a new life and given a new kind of work to do as ministers of a new covenant.

4. Break into pairs and discuss the following passages. What do you learn about the new life represented by the church?

- John 13:34-35

- Romans 6:4

- 2 Corinthians 3:6

- 2 Corinthians 5:17

- James 1:17-18

5. Read Matthew 5:1–6:18. How would you summarize the difference Jesus encourages his followers to adopt through his new teachings?

6. The church is instructed in Ephesians 4:17-32 and Colossians 3:1-25 to take off the old self and to put on the new self that has been made available through Christ. How would you summarize the old and new self?

7. What has this discussion revealed to you about who God is and how God works?

Missionary Imagination: *Risk Taking as a Contrast Community*

The missional communities studied in *Treasure in Clay Jars* found unique ways to be a new creation in the world around them, a contrast community that took risks instead of buying into the status quo. Some of the congregations practiced being present with the poor instead of living materialistically. Others exemplified a remarkable commitment to community formation instead of living individualistically. Many found unique ways to be creatively generous with their resources and to focus their ministries on the margins of society. They were all willing to love as Christ loved and suffer as Christ suffered so that others might know the love of God in real and tangible ways. Their actions and their deeds became a witness to a new kind of community.

8. What kind of witness is your group? In what ways is your witness strengthened by being a "contrast community"? In what ways is your witness perhaps weakened by conforming with the world?

9. Draw two pictures: one of the world around you and another of how your community can contrast that world.

10. It often takes courage to be different. Being a contrast community means taking risks and living a bit dangerously. What risks face your group, particularly if you live as a contrast community? How can you work together to face them?

11. Use the concepts and ideas you just discussed to update your model of the church as a missional community. What needs to be added to the model? Taken away? Modified?

12. Rewrite, add to or change your group covenant as you see fit based on the conversation you had during this session. Record your updated covenant here.

Before We Meet Again

- Continue to read and reflect on 1 Peter 2:4-12 or any other passage from this week's conversation. Record your thoughts here:

- Complete one of the following creative exercises. Be prepared to share your creation at the next group gathering.

  - In Acts 5 an angel of the Lord releases the apostles and tells them, "Go, stand in the temple courts . . . and tell the people all about this new life" (Acts 5:20). Read Acts 5 and then rewrite it as a story about God asking you to tell of the new life. Make sure to include how you would describe the new life the angel referred to.

  - Listen to the song "A New Way to Be Human" by Switchfoot and then write new lyrics that summarize the discussion you had regarding the church as the new creation of the Holy Spirit.

- Continue to study the image of the church as the new creation by reading paragraphs 34-43 of "The Nature and Mission of the Church" by the World Council of Churches (available online). You will find recommendations for additional resources at the end of this guide.

Session Six

LIVING AS THE
FELLOWSHIP OF THE FAITH

The final image of the church that helps to reveal its missionary nature is the image of fellowship in faith.

> The Church is the communion of those who, by means of their encounter with the Word, stand in a living relationship with God, who speaks to them and calls forth their trustful response; it is the communion of the faithful. This is the common vocation of every Christian and is exemplified by the faithful responsiveness of Mary to the angel of the annunciation: "Here I am, the servant of the Lord; let it be with me according to your word" (Lk 1:38).[20]

Mary's words unite the community. Through faith individuals in the Christian community encounter God, and through faith they are united in their response of "Here I am, the servant of the Lord; let it be with me according to your word" (Lk 1:38 NRSV).

Faith unites diverse individuals through common belief and through a common response to those beliefs. United under the declaration of faith that Jesus is Lord, Christians are formed together into a community that seeks to live out the implications of the lordship of Jesus together. The community of faith shares a common vocation to participate in the mission of God through faith; it is a community that acts and works together to serve that mission, and that mutually encourages and provides accountability for all members as they seek to grow in their faith together. The church is a fellowship of faith that is united in love for God and bonded together through its missionary response to God's love.

Share your thoughts, reflections and creative activities from session 5.

Dwelling in the Word

- Begin in prayer, inviting the Spirit to guide your group as you dwell in the text.

- Read aloud 1 Peter 2:4-12.

- After the reading has been completed, allow a few moments of silence to reflect on the passage and what stands out to you.

- Break into pairs (preferably with someone you don't know well) and discuss the following questions. Use this time to practice listening to each other as well as to the text.

  - What in the text captured your imagination?

  - What question would you most like to ask a biblical scholar?

- Gather once again as a large group and share your partners' responses.

- Review these responses and discuss: What might God be up to in the passage for us today?

Contextual Analysis

1. How do you think the people in your context would describe the community that they experience? What name would you give to their experience of community?

2. What are the similarities and differences you see between the community your context experiences and the community the church experiences as the fellowship of faith?

3. What difference would experiencing the fellowship of faith make in the lives of the people in your mission context?

Theological Reflection: *God Unites His People Through New Relationships*

First John is about the fellowship of the believers with God and with one another. First John 1:1–2:27 describes the foundation on which Christians have fellowship with God and one another. First John 3:1–5:21 describes the lifestyle that ought to define the fellowship.

4. Break into pairs, with some reading and answering part A and others part B below.

A. Read 1 John 1:1–2:27. What is the foundation for Christian fellowship?

B. Read 1 John 3:1-24 and 4:7-21. What behaviors ought to define the community?

5. Scripture contains interesting case studies in how the fellowship of faith actually functions in its day-to-day existence. Break into pairs to read the following texts as case studies. What principles can you draw from the text?

Romans 14:1–15:16

Acts 4:23–5:11

6. Philippians 2:1-18 grounds the nature and lifestyle of the fellowship of faith in the nature and lifestyle of God. Read this Scripture. What do you learn about God? How does this help you understand what it means to be the church?

Missionary Imagination: *Biblical Formation and Discipleship*

The missional congregation, according to the research in *Treasure in Clay Jars*, is a fellowship of faith in that it is biblically centered *and* focused on being formed into a missional community by the Word. This combination of Bible centeredness and community formation, according to the author, is quite rare in the West.

It is possible to be biblically centered, to expect and to experience biblical preaching, and not to be a church that acknowledges, much less practices, its missional calling. This is the crisis and dilemma of much of the Western church. It is possible to study the Scriptures in such a way that its central emphasis upon formation is missed. It is possible to hear the gospel primarily in terms of what it does for me, or for you. It is possible to take the Bible seriously, persuaded that it is primarily about one's personal salvation. It is possible to preach the Bible in such a way that the needs of persons are met but the formation of the whole community for its witness in the world is not emphasized. It is, in short, possible to be Bible-centered and not wholeheartedly missional.[21]

7. On a scale of 1-10, how well does biblical formation translate into

missional community formation in your life? Your group? Your church? What would move it one point higher?

8. What practices help ensure that biblical formation is missional?

"The Nature and Mission of Church" describes the practices that characterize the fellowship of faith:

> Visible and tangible signs of the new life of communion are expressed in receiving and sharing the faith of the apostles; breaking and sharing the Eucharistic bread; praying with and for one another and for the needs of the world; serving one another in love; participating in each other's joys and sorrows; giving material aid; proclaiming and witnessing to the good news in mission and working together for justice and peace. The communion of the Church consists not of independent individuals but of persons in community, all of whom contribute to its flourishing.[22]

9. Reflect on the list. How well do you think "The Nature and Mission of the Church" describes the fellowship of faith? How well does its definition describe your group?

10. Finalize the model of the missional community that you have been building throughout all six sessions of this conversation guide. How would you describe your model to someone who was not familiar with it?

11. Revisit the covenant/confession you wrote together as a group during previous sessions. Rewrite, add to or change the covenant as you see fit based on the conversation you had during this session. Record your updated covenant here.

Final Assignments

- Continue to read and reflect on 1 Peter 2:4-12 or any of the other passages from this week's conversation. Record your thoughts here:

- Plan a dinner party with your group. Use the party to celebrate your experience and imagine how you will move forward as a missional community.

- Continue to study the image of the church as the fellowship of faith by reading paragraphs 24-33 "The Nature and Mission of the Church" by the World Council of Churches (available online). You will find recommendations for additional resources at the end of this guide.

- It is often said that teaching is the best form of learning. Therefore, identify two to six other people in your life who you could take through the material covered during your study or the key learning you gleaned from the conversations. Use this conversation guide or create your own process to take your friends through a learning journey with you.

Appendix

TIPS FOR HAVING GREAT
SMALL GROUP GATHERINGS

The following tips were gleaned from my experience in small group ministry. Practice these over the course of your time together, but know they are not exhaustive. Space has been left at the end for your group to add its own tips for having great small group gatherings.

TIP 1: *Be Prepared*

Group gatherings flourish when folks come prepared. If there is one person designated to lead or facilitate the gathering, that person should be in prayer throughout the week, asking God's Spirit to lead him or her and to be present at the gathering. The leader or facilitator should also personally work through the material a couple of times so he or she can create a gathering that flows smoothly and achieves the desired objectives.

It is also important for group members to come prepared. Their preparation includes completing midweek assignments, bringing re-

quired materials, opening their minds to what God might want to say
and opening their lives to where the Spirit might want to lead.

TIP 2: *Foster Habits That Create Good Conversation and Discussion*

There is a reason these guides have been titled Forge Guides for Missional Conversation. They are meant to *create conversation* about
living missionally! It is important that groups foster habits that help
create good conversation. These habits include:

- Directing discussion toward all group members, not just the facilitator. Often when someone responds to a question, he or she will
  look at the person who asked the question. Group members should
  look at and interact with *one another* while giving their responses,
  not just the leader.

- Avoid the silent head nod, which is one of the biggest conversation
  killers. Unfortunately, it is a hard habit to break. However, when
  someone shares or offers a response, the group should work to give
  more of a response than the silent nod. Perhaps someone could ask
  a question, share their own insight, request for the person to say
  more or even just say thanks.

- Ask good questions and follow-up questions. The questions provided for you in the conversation guides will hopefully be effective
  at sparking conversations. It is imperative that the group does not
  merely answer the questions provided but asks new questions as
  the conversation continues. Asking new questions is a good indi-
  cation that group members are listening to one another and taking
  an active interest in what is being said.

- Draw answers out of each participant. One of the cardinal sins of
  teaching or leading a discussion is to answer your own question to
  avoid the awkward silence. If a question is asked and no one answers after you have allowed for a comfortable time of silence, con-

sider repeating or rephrasing the question. Also consider calling on a specific person to answer. Most of the time the person called on will have something insightful to share. I often am amazed at what the quietest people in groups have to say when a leader calls on them to specifically share. As a last resort, suggest that the group come back to the question later, or give time for individuals to share with their neighbor before sharing with everyone.

- As much as possible, affirm what others say. People feel affirmed when their thoughts are repeated or referred to later in the discussion. When people feel affirmed, they are more likely to continue to participate in the conversation.

- Clarify or summarize what has been said. Sometimes a group member will offer a long answer or get sidetracked onto a different discussion. It is often helpful for the group leader or another member to summarize what has been said, even asking for clarity if necessary. This clarifying practice will help keep the conversation moving in a focused direction.

TIP 3: *Share Leadership and Always Give People Something to Contribute*

Small groups flourish when all members are given a chance to lead on a regular basis and when all members are expected to contribute to each gathering. Rotate leadership and facilitating responsibilities while working through this guide if at all possible. Always try to find ways to ensure everyone is bringing something to contribute, whether an activity to plan or simply a snack to share.

TIP 4: *Encourage and Affirm One Another as Much as Possible*

A little bit of affirmation goes such a long way in small groups. Telling someone he or she had a good idea, did a good job leading, brought good energy to the group or made a nice snack will encourage the person to continue to participate in group gatherings in important ways. Groups that are able to identify each other's strengths and to encourage those strengths to be used more will be full of life, energy and possibility.

TIP 5: *Create Space for Feedback*

Group gatherings will be better over the long run if the group can create a regular rhythm of giving and receiving feedback about group gatherings. Allowing all members to give input or offer ideas for future gatherings will increase ownership and help craft an experience unique to the group.

RECOMMENDED RESOURCES
FOR FURTHER STUDY

The following resources can be used to supplement your "Before We Meet Again" assignments that ask you to keep studying the image of the church studied during each session.

Session 1 Readings

The Church as the Elect People of God

- Paul Minear, *Images of the Church in the New Testament* (Louisville: Westminster John Knox Press, 2004), pp. 66-104. Or study on your own the use of the following images in the Bible that Minear identifies as related to the elect people of God: the church as the people of God, Israel (a chosen race, a holy nation, twelve tribes, the patriarchs, circumcision, Abraham's sons, the exodus, house of David, remnant, the elect) flock, lambs who rule, the Holy City, the holy temple, priesthood, sacrifice, aroma and festivals.

- Paragraphs 9-18 of "The Nature and Mission of the Church: A Stage on the Way to a Common Statement," Faith and Order Paper 198 (2005), available online.

Discerning Missional Vocation

- Lois Y. Barrett, *Treasure in Clay Jars: Patterns in Missional Faith-fulness* (Grand Rapids: Eerdmans, 2004), pp. 33-58.

- Darrell L. Guder et al., "Missional Vocation: Called and Sent to Represent the Reign of God," in *Missional Church: A Vision for the Sending of the Church in North America*, ed. Darrell L. Guder (Grand Rapids: Eerdmans, 1998), pp. 77-109.

- Craig Van Gelder, *The Ministry of the Missional Church* (Grand Rapids: Baker, 2007).

- Patrick R. Keifert, *We Are Here Now: A New Missional Era* (Eagle, ID: Allelon, 2006).

Session 2 Readings

The Church as the Pilgrim People of God

- Paul Minear, *Images of the Church in the New Testament* (Louisville: Westminster John Knox Press, 2004), pp. 60-62.

- Paragraphs 19, 43-47 of "The Nature and Mission of the Church: A Stage on the Way to a Common Statement," Faith and Order Paper 198 (2005), available online.

- Vatican II, *Ad Gentes*, www.vatican.va/archive/hist_councils/ii_vatican_council/documents/vat-ii_decree_19651207_ad-gentes_en.html.

Pointing Toward the Reign of God

- Lois Y. Barrett, *Treasure in Clay Jars: Patterns in Missional Faith-fulness* (Grand Rapids: Eerdmans, 2004), pp. 126-38.

- Darrell L. Guder et al., "Missional Vocation: Called and Sent to Represent the Reign of God," in *Missional Church: A Vision for the*

Sending of the Church in North America, ed. Darrell L. Guder (Grand Rapids: Eerdmans, 1998), pp. 77-109.

- Craig Van Gelder, *The Essence of the Church: A Community Created by the Spirit* (Grand Rapids: Baker, 2000), pp. 73-100.

Session 3 Readings

The Church as the Body of Christ

- Paul Minear, *Images of the Church in the New Testament* (Louisville: Westminster John Knox Press, 2004), pp. 173-220. Or study on your own the terms that relate to the image of the church as the body of Christ as identified by Minear: body (members or the head), body of life, members of Christ, the body and the blood, the diversities of ministries, spiritual body, head of cosmic spirits, head of the church, the body of this head, the unity of Jews and Gentiles, the growth of the body, and the fullness of God.

- Paragraphs 20-21 of "The Nature and Mission of the Church: A Stage on the Way to a Common Statement," Faith and Order Paper 198 (2005), available online.

Practices That Demonstrate God's Intent for the World

- Lois Y. Barrett, *Treasure in Clay Jars: Patterns in Missional Faithfulness* (Grand Rapids: Eerdmans, 2004), pp. 84-99.

- Darrell L. Guder et al., "Missional Structures: The Particular Community," in *Missional Church: A Vision for the Sending of the Church in North America*, ed. Darrell L. Guder (Grand Rapids: Eerdmans, 1998), pp. 221-47.

- Milfred Minatrea, *Shaped by God's Heart: The Passion and Practices of Missional Churches* (San Francisco: Jossey-Bass, 2004).

Session 4 Readings

The Church as the Temple of the Holy Spirit

- Paul Minear, *Images of the Church in the New Testament* (Louisville: Westminster John Knox Press, 2004), pp. 49-50, 91-98, 125-27, 165-67, 213-17. Or study on your own the terms that relate to the image of the church as the temple of the Holy Spirit: God's building, the Holy City, the holy temple, God's glory, household of God and the fullness of God.

- Paragraphs 22-23 of "The Nature and Mission of the Church: A Stage on the Way to a Common Statement," Faith and Order Paper 198 (2005), available online.

Dependence on the Holy Spirit

- Lois Y. Barrett, *Treasure in Clay Jars: Patterns in Missional Faithfulness* (Grand Rapids: Eerdmans, 2004), pp. 117-25.

- Darrell L. Guder et al., "Missional Community: Cultivating Communities of the Holy Spirit," in *Missional Church: A Vision for the Sending of the Church in North America*, ed. Darrell L. Guder (Grand Rapids: Eerdmans, 1998), pp. 142-82.

- Craig Van Gelder, *The Ministry of the Missional Church* (Grand Rapids: Baker, 2007), pp. 15-68.

Session 5 Readings

The Church as the New Creation

- Paul Minear, *Images of the Church in the New Testament* (Louisville: Westminster John Knox Press, 2004), pp. 105-35. Or study on your own the terms that relate to the image of the church as the new creation as identified by Minear: the new creation, first fruits, the new humanity, the last Adam, the Son of Man, the kingdom of

God, fighters against Satan, Sabbath rest, the coming age, God's glory, light, the name, life, the tree of life, communion in the Holy Spirit and the bond of love.

- Paragraphs 34-43 of "The Nature and Mission of the Church: A Stage on the Way to a Common Statement," Faith and Order Paper 198 (2005), available online.

Risk Taking as a Contrast Community

- Lois Y. Barrett, *Treasure in Clay Jars: Patterns in Missional Faithfulness* (Grand Rapids: Eerdmans, 2004), pp. 74-83.

- Darrell L. Guder et al., "Missional Witness: The Church as Apostle to the World," in *Missional Church: A Vision for the Sending of the Church in North America*, ed. Darrell L. Guder (Grand Rapids: Eerdmans, 1998), pp. 221-47.

- Michael Frost and Alan Hirsch, *The Faith of Leap: Embracing a Theology of Risk, Adventure & Courage* (Grand Rapids: Baker, 2011).

Session 6 Readings

The Church as the Fellowship of Faith

- Paul Minear, *Images of the Church in the New Testament* (Louisville: Westminster John Knox Press, 2004), pp. 136-72. Or study on your own the terms that relate to the image of the church as the fellowship of faith as identified by Minear: the sanctified, the faithful, the justified, followers, disciples, road, coming and going, witness community, confessors, slaves, friends, servants, "with," edification, household of God, sons of God and brotherhood.

- Paragraphs 24-33 of "The Nature and Mission of the Church: A Stage on the Way to a Common Statement," Faith and Order Paper 198 (2005), available online.

Biblical Formation and Discipleship

- Lois Y. Barrett, *Treasure in Clay Jars: Patterns in Missional Faithfulness* (Grand Rapids: Eerdmans, 2004), pp. 59-73.

- Dietrich Bonhoeffer, *Life Together* (New York: Harper & Row, 1954).

- Mike Breen and Steve Cockram, *Building a Discipling Culture* (Grand Rapids: Zondervan, 2009).

* * *

If you would like to broaden your missional imagination even further than you have already done through this study guide, the following resources will help you.

1. "A Brief History of the Missional Church Movement." This short essay describes the growth of the missional church movement from the World Missionary Conference in Edinburgh (1910) through today, identifying a variety of sources that have funded the movement. You can find this essay online at www.ivpress.com.

2. "Helpful Resources for Developing Missional Imagination." This list of resources is given to everyone who plays a leadership role in the Forge Mission Training Network so that they can expand their own imaginations for mission and help others do the same. You can view the list at www.ivpress.com. For more information on the books, you can view my list at www.worldcat.org/profiles/luthercml3/lists/2934221.

Notes

[1]Alan Hirsch, "Defining Missional," *Leadership Journal*, fall 2008, www.christianityto day.com/le/2008/fall/17.20.html.

[2]"Dwelling in the Word" is a practice developed and taught to me by Dr. Patrick Keifert of Church Innovations (www.churchinnovations.org). The instructions provided are a slightly modified version of the guide provided in Patrick Keifert and Pat Taylor Ellison, *Dwelling in the Word: A Pocket Handbook* (Minneapolis: Church Innovations Institute, 2011). For more on Dwelling in the Word, visit www.churchinnovations.org/06_about/dwelling.html.

[3]David H. Kelsey, *To Understand God Truly: What's Theological About a Theological School?* (Louisville: Westminster/John Knox Press, 1992).

[4]Paul Minear, *Images of the Church in the New Testament* (Louisville: Westminster John Knox Press, 2004), p. 67.

[5]Lois Y. Barrett, *Treasure in Clay Jars: Patterns in Missional Faithfulness* (Grand Rapids: Eerdmans, 2004), p. 37.

[6]World Council of Churches, "The Nature and Mission of the Church: A Stage on the Way to a Common Statement," Faith and Order Paper 198 (2005): 29.

[7]Barrett, *Treasure in Clay Jars*, pp. 36-37.

[8]Darrell L. Guder, "Missional Structures: The Particular Community," in *Missional Church: A Vision for the Sending of the Church in North America*, ed. Darrell L. Guder (Grand Rapids: Eerdmans, 1998), p. 236.

[9]Lesslie Newbigin, *The Household of God: Lectures on the Nature of the Church* (New York: Friendship Press, 1954), p. 18.

[10]World Council of Churches, "The Nature and Mission of the Church: A Stage on the Way to a Common Statement," Faith and Order Paper 198 (2005).

[11]Phil Needham, *Community in Mission: A Salvationist Ecclesiology* (London: Salvation Army, 1987), p. 35.

[12]Craig Van Gelder, *The Essence of the Church: A Community Created by the Spirit* (Grand Rapids: Baker, 2000), p. 139.

[13]Lois Y. Barrett, *Treasure in Clay Jars: Patterns in Missional Faithfulness* (Grand Rapids: Eerdmans, 2004), p. 128.

[14]Paul Minear, *Images of the Church in the New Testament* (Louisville: Westminster John Knox Press, 2004), p. 211.

[15]Craig Van Gelder, *The Essence of the Church: A Community Created by the Spirit* (Grand Rapids: Baker, 2000), p. 100.

[16]Ibid.

[17]Lois Y. Barrett, *Treasure in Clay Jars: Patterns in Missional Faithfulness* (Grand Rapids: Eerdmans, 2004), p. 84.

[18]Dietrich Bonhoeffer, *Life Together: The Classic Exploration of Christian Community* (New York: HarperCollins, 1978), p. 24.

[19]Lois Y. Barrett, *Treasure in Clay Jars: Patterns in Missional Faithfulness* (Grand Rapids: Eerdmans, 2004), p. 119.

[20]World Council of Churches, "The Nature and Mission of the Church: A Stage on the Way to a Common Statement," Faith and Order Paper 198 (2005): 4.

[21]Lois Y. Barrett, *Treasure in Clay Jars: Patterns in Missional Faithfulness* (Grand Rapids: Eerdmans, 2004), p. 60.

[22]World Council of Churches, "The Nature and Mission of the Church," p. 9.

Forge Guides
for Missional Conversation

COMMUNITY: *Living as the People of God*
MISSION: *Living for the Purposes of God*
POWER: *Living by the Spirit of God*
VISION: *Living Under the Promises of God*
CULTURE: *Living in the Places of God*

How can God's people give witness to his kingdom in an increasingly post-Christian culture? How can the church recover its true mission in the face of a world in need? Forge America exists to help birth and nurture the missional church in America and beyond. Books published by InterVarsity Press that bear the Forge imprint will also serve that purpose.

Forge Books from InterVarsity Press

Creating a Missional Culture, JR Woodward

Forge Guides for Missional Conversation (set of five), Scott Nelson

The Missional Quest, Lance Ford and Brad Brisco

More Than Enchanting, Jo Saxton

The Story of God, the Story of Us, Sean Gladding

For more information on Forge America, to apply for a
Forge residency, or to find or start a Forge hub in your area,
visit **www.forgeamerica.com**

For more information about Forge books from
InterVarsity Press, including forthcoming releases,
visit **www.ivpress.com/forge**